Self-Hypnosis
How to Feel Relaxed
Achieve Your Goals
and
Stay Motivated

the rendering of legal, financial, medical or professional advice. The content of this book has been derived from various sources. Please consult a licensed professional before attempting any techniques outlined in this book.

By reading this document, the reader agrees that under no circumstances is the author responsible for any losses, direct or indirect, which are incurred as a result of the use of information contained within this document, including, but not limited to, —errors, omissions, or inaccuracies.

Table of Contents

Introduction

To understand self-hypnosis, you first need to learn about hypnosis. What is hypnosis? Also referred to as hypnotherapy, hypnosis uses intense focus and concentration through guided relaxation methods to reach a 'trance' or a heightened state of awareness.

A hypnotist uses suggestions to get you into a hypnotic state. Examples of these suggestions include:

- Relax your entire body from head to toe.
- Imagine the most peaceful and relaxed place you have ever been to.
- Imagine hearing your beloved grandmother's voice.

When you focus on any of these or other suggestions given by the hypnotizer, then you tend to reach a hypnotic 'trance.' And if this process is done over a sustained period of time, like say 10-15 minutes, your mind tends to reach deeper levels of consciousness.

By the way, hypnosis is not something mysterious and indefinable. If you notice all the great marketing and PR campaigns or political and religious propaganda are working on the idea of hypnotizing people into believing something. Most of us fall for these concepts, right?

Some people use this concept to mislead, delude, and misguide us while some others use it for our good. So, hypnosis works and therefore can be used for your own good through the practice of self-hypnosis. Self-hypnosis is, therefore, using the 'power' of hypnosis on yourself to make positive changes in your life. By using self-hypnosis, you are suggesting certain desirable things for yourself.

The original word for hypnosis was mesmerism drawn from the root word 'to mesmerize.' So, have you found yourself totally mesmerized by the sound and sight of sea waves, a crackling fire, ripples in a pond, or the flame of a candle? This experience is nothing but self-hypnosis.

During such an experience, you would have felt a profound sense of relaxation and would have been so lost in thought that you would not have been aware of the world around you. When you intentionally put yourself in this state of mind, then it is called self-hypnosis.

Additionally, many experts believe that the term 'self-hypnosis' is redundant because no one can hypnotize you until you allow it to happen. Primarily, we can only hypnotize ourselves and only when we want to. A hypnotherapist only facilitates the entire process. Therefore, even hypnotherapy done by another person is essentially self-hypnosis.

How Does Self-Hypnosis Work?

Most of us undergo different states of consciousness and moods right through the day. In one instant, we feel happy and ecstatic, and the next moment (for no explicable reason) we feel sad and depressed.

For example, on any given day, suppose you are feeling great and happy with everything. Now, a call comes from your broker telling you that the stocks you bought have crashed, and you have lost a considerable amount of money. Your mood and thoughts undergo drastic changes immediately.

Now, suppose, after a little while, you get another call saying you won a big lottery. Again, your mood undergoes significant changes from sadness and depression to happiness and joy.

Each of these moods is actually little pockets of hypnosis, and therefore there is no one hypnotic state to reach unless you have achieved enlightenment like the Buddha. No physical change has come over you during any of these changing moods. Only your mental image about the world and yourself have altered.

People in a hypnotic, receptive trance can get a rash if it is suggested to them that they have touched poison ivy. People in a hypnotic trance can shiver if it is suggested to them they are standing naked in the cold outside. How does this happen? Because there is a direct link between the mental images formed in your mind and their effects on your body. Using this body-mind connection, you can use self-hypnosis to improve the quality of life or bring about other positive changes.

Benefits of Self-Hypnosis

Self-hypnosis is slowly gathering momentum as a powerful tool to improve one's own life. It helps you take control of and makes you accountable for your own life. Each of us can delve deep into our consciousness and access power and abilities that are not available at a cursory level.

Self-hypnosis helps you enhance your life successes, bring in more positivity, and make transformational changes. You can use the powerful tool of self-hypnosis for the following benefits:

- For a stress-free, relaxing experience to get rid of fatigue and tiredness.

- For self-improvement.

- To get rid of negative self-talk, which, in turn, gives you, increased control of your mind.
- To reduce anxiety and stress.

- For anger management.
- To help you overcome the pain of childhood and past traumas.
- For improved emotional well-being.
- For self-actualization which is nothing but reaching your best potential.
- To improve success in your life and to achieve your goals.
- To boost self-esteem and self-confidence.
- To help you gain better control over your thoughts and emotions.

Read on to see how you can use self-hypnosis for all the above benefits.

Chapter One: Self-Hypnosis for Relaxation and Stress Management

Self-hypnosis is a powerful tool to relax and manage everyday stresses. Remember that self-hypnosis is not magic, and will not give overnight miracles. It requires belief and faith followed with consistent practice until your mind can reach a receptive, trance stage so that you can make suggestions connected to stress management and relaxation.

Importance of Relaxation and Stress Management

Proper relaxation is crucial for long-term happiness and health. Unresolved stress leads to multiple health problems including lowered immunity, digestive problems, chronic pain-related complaints, and much more. It is therefore imperative that you should find ways to relax and manage stress.

When you relax, your body responds in the following ways all of which are beneficial for long-term mental, physical, and emotional health:

- Your breathing gets deeper and slower.
- Your heart rate reduces.
- The blood flow to all parts of your body including your extremities increases.
- Your hormone levels are balanced.

- Your metabolism achieves optimal levels.

Here are some pointers to focus on if you want to make a success of self-hypnosis therapy:

- You must have a deep desire to try self-hypnosis.
- You should not be excessively skeptical. It is not an exact science yet. But, many people have tried it and found success.
- You should not be afraid of hypnosis. Remember no one can control your mind until you allow it.
- Don't over-analyze the underlying scientific and technical data. Keep an open mind and start your self-hypnosis journey.

Also, get yourself prepared for the reasons for undergoing self-hypnosis. Write down the messages and suggestions you want to give yourself when you are in the receptive, trance-like state. What ideas do you want to plant in your subconscious mind? Create short, powerful statements that you can repeat to yourself when you reach the hypnotic state. Here are some tips on how to create compelling, suggestive statements for self-hypnosis:

- The statement has to honest and genuine. The success of the self-hypnosis technique depends on how deeply and honestly you aspire to do what you want. You cannot really implant goals and purposes that you are not very keen on achieving.

- Your statement should be a powerful and positive one.
- And finally, don't complicate your sentences. Keep them simple so that it is easy to recall them during the hypnotic trance. For example, 'I am feeling relaxed' or 'I am free from stress.' Here are some more examples of persuasive and simple self-suggestions for relaxation and stress management:

  - o I take deeper and more relaxed breaths than before.
  - o I am at peace with myself.
  - o My thoughts are under my control.
  - o I am happy and comfortable.
  - o I am calm, relaxed, and stress-free.
  - o I become increasingly relaxed with every breath I take.

Steps for Relaxation Self-Hypnosis

Use the following steps to create a self-hypnotic state and then give yourself stress reduction and relaxation suggestions:

- First, relax your body by sitting in a comfortable position. You can start by focusing on your breath so that your body and mind begin the relaxation process.

- Identify an object to focus your thoughts on. Typically, this object should be placed on the wall on a slightly higher level than your eye level.

- Clear your mind of all thoughts and ideas, and focus only on that one object. This step is going to be the hardest to perfect. Be ready to practice a lot before achieving some semblance of perfection of being able to focus only on the object while clearing your mind of all other thoughts.

- Pay attention to your eyelids, and imagine them becoming heavy. Now, picture the heavy eyelids closing slowly. Now, shift your focus to your breath as your eyes close. Focus on breathing evenly and deeply.

- Tell yourself that you are becoming increasingly relaxed with each exhalation. Slow down your breathing and feel your body relax with every breath.

- Imagine an object like a pendulum moving with amazing regularity from one side to another. Follow the regular motion of the pendulum in your mind's eye.

- Next, in your mind, count backward from ten slowly and monotonously. After each number say 'I am relaxed.' For example:

  - 10 – I am relaxed
  - 9 – I am relaxed
  - 8 – I am relaxed
  - 7 -
  - 6 -
  - 5 -

- Believe in your ability to become relaxed when you complete this exercise. Repeat this self-believing statement in your mind.

- When you reach the self-hypnotized state, then it is time to focus on the relaxation and stress-reducing statements that you have prepared for yourself.

- Focus on each of them, repeat them in your mind, and remain relaxed and stress-free.

- When you feel satiated, come out of your hypnotic state after clearing your mind. Use these steps for this purpose:

- Slowly count forward from one to ten. After each count, give a powerful self-suggestion which could be something like, 'When I wake up, I will feel completed relaxed and stress-free.'

- When you reach number 10, you will feel fully awake, and completely relaxed. Gradually, allow your conscious mind to catch up with the external surroundings and the events of the day.

The trick is to repeatedly practice and perfect the art of achieving a self-hypnotic state. The more you practice, the easier it will become for you to quickly and effectively reach the 'trance' state so that your mind is at its receptive best to receive self-suggestions for relaxation and stress management.

Chapter Two: Self-Hypnosis for Motivation and Achieving Success

The lack of motivation is one of the primary reasons that prevents us from achieving success. Our lack of motivation is largely driven by preconditioned thoughts and ideas like fear of failure or unpleasantness of a particular task or anything else.

These preconditioned ideas are deeply embedded in our subconscious minds creating seemingly insurmountable obstacles for motivation to find its way into our lives. That is to say, we have trained our minds to work against our needs and desires rather than toward our success.

The inner voice in our heads becomes our biggest critic and a bad influence creating negative thoughts that continuously tell us not to try something because of various baseless reasons. Here too, self-hypnosis can be of immense help.

Self-hypnosis can direct our minds to convert these negative influences into positive ones so that our mind is aligned with our life instead of being against it. With self-hypnosis, you can train your mind to respond positively to adversities and challenges, which, in turn, builds motivation. But before that, let us try and understand the lack of motivation a little more.

Signs of the Lack of Motivation

It is important to remember that in the context of this book, we are not talking about the lack of motivation to clean your car on a Sunday morning or doing some other chore in and around your house. We are talking about that aspect of motivation which when not present in sufficient quantities negatively impacts your life, career, relationships, and over time, can lead to depression and anxiety.

However, it is equally important to remember that the lack of motivation to do the first type of work (the routine, and yes, many times, tedious chores) continues unresolved for a long time, then it can get converted into losing motivation for living life itself.

So, you must recognize this element and work towards doing the boring but important chores too. Here are some unmissable signs that tell you loud and clear that you lack motivation:

- Losing interest quickly in whatever you do.
- Putting off work and critical assignments.
- Not completing tasks well.
- Losing track of your life purpose and goals.
- Feeling a sense of inadequacy.
- Feeling gloomy, depressed, and anxious.

How to Use Self-Hypnosis for Motivation

You can use the power of self-hypnosis to convert your negative thoughts into positive ones that keep your motivation levels high and keeps you on the right track to achieve your goals. Follow these steps:

- Sit or lie down in a relaxed, comfortable position.

- Close your eyes and focus on your breath for a couple of minutes until you feel completely relaxed and comfortable.

- Then, imagine yourself in a hallway standing in front of an escalator that is going in the downward direction.

- Watch the movement of the escalator and everything else about it. Pay attention to the steps as they seem to flow downwards. Focus on the handles on either side, which you can hold on to for your safety.

- Then, slowly imagine yourself getting on to the escalator, and moving downwards. Feel yourself relaxing more and more as the escalator smoothly moves down.

- As you move downwards, tell yourself that the time has come for you to increase your motivation levels so that you can achieve your goals.

- Confidently, tell yourself that you always knew that the time for self-realization and self-actualization will come in your life, and this little exercise is the first step towards it.

- Tell yourself that the time to take control of your life has come, and you are ready for it.

- Now, you have reached the end of the escalator. Imagine a wide, open, and airy room. You can see your favorite chair in one corner of the room. Go sit on that chair, and close your eyes.

- Make yourself as comfortable as possible on your cozy, favorite chair.

Imagine the goal you desire and visualize yourself achieving that goal successfully. Visualize a detailed scene of when you achieve that goal including what you feel, hear, see, and other sensations.

Now, in your imagination think back to the first step you took towards building motivation to achieve your goal. Tell yourself how easy it is to get what you want, provided you want it deeply enough.

Remember that the most difficult aspect of achieving the goal is to get started. Once you take the first step, then everything simply falls into place.

Finding the motivation to take the second step is easy because of the success of taking the first one, and so forth. With each succeeding step you take towards achieving your goal, you will see the path becoming increasingly clear of obstacles and challenges keeping your motivation levels high.

As you soak in the experience of this self-hypnotic visualization, repeat the following motivation-building suggestions to yourself:

- I am motivated to overcome challenges and move ahead on the path of success.
- Fear is nothing but a feeling and has no power over me.
- I feel energized and motivated to do everything it takes to succeed.
- I have the power and determination and power to convert my dreams into reality.
- Every step I take towards my goals gives me the motivation to take the next step.

Remember you and only you control your life and its events. So, sit on the driver's seat and go where your heart and mind want to take you. So, live your dreams, and don't allow the lack of motivation to stop your progress.

Chapter Three: Self-Hypnosis to Eliminate Bad Habits

Let us begin by reiterating the way self-hypnosis works. It is the process of making powerful suggestions to your subconscious mind, which, in turn, drives your conscious mind and physical body to achieve what you want. This method is therefore found to be very useful in treating and overcoming bad habits including addictions.

Some undesirable behaviors are easier to get rid of than others. If you can summon your willpower, then it might be possible to eliminate certain bad habits from your life. However, if you see that despite your best efforts at summoning all your willpower and logical thought process, you are unable to get rid of some of the bad habits from your life, then you must know that the problem goes deeper than you thought.

Logical thinking skills and willpower happen at the level of the conscious mind. The elements that have lasting behavioral changes reside at the subconscious level, which holds beliefs, emotions, habits, values, intuition, and the power of your imagination reside. Therefore, if you want to get rid of some bad habits, you need to connect to your subconscious mind, which is what self-hypnosis helps you do.

It is important to remember that self-hypnosis is not a magic cure. It would be foolhardy to undergo one session of self-hypnosis and expect to come away completely cured. No, it does not work like that. Remember that in self-hypnosis, you are the therapist as well as the patient. In the same way as the therapist works hard to connect with his or her patient, you must endeavor to connect with your subconscious so that you can root out bad habits through powerful self-suggestions.

You can use self-hypnosis to cure your bad habits and addictions with the following intents:

- To reduce the agonizing effects of withdrawal symptoms through self-suggestions.
- To create aversion and hatred to bad habits and undesirable behaviors including addictions and drug abuse.
- To develop meaningful and deep conversations with your subconscious mind without the judgmental attitude of your conscious mind.

Self-Hypnosis Steps to Eliminate Bad Habits and Behaviors

Before you begin, focus on yourself and rate your stress level on a scale of 1 to 10; 1 is for feeling completely relaxed, and 10 is for being totally stressed out.

Step 1 – Sit comfortably on a chair. Place your hands on your lap and make sure your feet are firmly on the ground. Breathe slowly and deliberately inhaling through your left nostril for four counts and exhaling through your right nostril for eight counts. Do this until you feel stable and strong and are ready to move on.

Step 2 – Visualize your favorite color flowing into your body through your head, passing through every nook and corner of your body, and then exiting out from your feet into the ground beneath. This visualization is an excellent way to remove stresses from your body. Imagine the flow of your favorite color rinsing out and eliminating stresses from your body and mind.

Step 3 – Keep your eyes closed, and count backward from 10 to 1, and at each number, remember to tell yourself that you are getting increasingly relaxed.

Step 4 – When you are deeply in the hypnotic 'trance' state, repeat the following affirmation: I am safe, relaxed, and in this state. And then, use this step for getting rid of different bad habits. For example:

- If you want to get to bed early every day, practice this step with the affirmation, 'When I go to bed early, I feel healthy, happy, and charged with energy to achieve my goals.' Visualize yourself going to bed early and rising early and tackling life challenges with added vigor.

- If you want to stick to a healthy diet plan, you can use this affirmation, 'With this healthy diet plan, I will feel fit and ready to take control of my life in my hands.' Visualize yourself consuming healthy meals and saying no to unhealthy foods. Imagine achieving your weight loss goals through this process.

- If you want to give up smoking, 'Giving up smoking is the best gift to myself and my loved ones.' Visualize a life when you do not give in to smoking. Think of the happiness on the faces of your loved ones when you reach this smoke-free state.

Step 5 – Remember to focus on your breath as you go through Step 4 and feel the relaxation and stress-free feeling surround your body and mind. Allow your subconscious mind to come to the forefront so that you can connect with it and make powerful suggestions to it. Even after you come out of this self-hypnotic session, you will be able to carry forth this relaxing experience right through the day even as you feel charged up to keep out the bad habits from your life.

Step 6 – Now, count from 1 to 10, and you move forward, slowly get out of your hypnotic zone and become aware of the external surroundings. When you are completely out of your self-hypnosis session, rate your stress level, and notice the difference between this and the level when you started the session.

Chapter Four: Self-Hypnosis for Self-Improvement and Emotional Well-Being

As you already know hypnosis is an altered state of mind in which you can access your subconscious mind to make powerful suggestions. If these suggestions are based on self-improvement, then you are bound to see yourself become a better person in every way; emotionally, physically and mentally.

Our subconscious mind is the repository of all our beliefs based on which we lead our lives. Therefore, if you are unhappy with your present life, then you must sow the right kind of seeds in your subconscious mind so that your life will improve and you can achieve self-actualization.

Through self-hypnosis, you are effectively putting your conscious mind to sleep so that you can directly access its powers as well as make powerful suggestions for positive life changes.

One of the biggest elements that prevent us from self-actualization is our limiting beliefs that many of us carry in our heads since our childhood. Here is a classic example of how some deep-seated limiting beliefs prevent our growth.

Calves are tethered with strong ropes to stakes so that they don't run away. These small animals are unable to free themselves no matter how hard they try. They give up attempting to free themselves after a few months. After a couple of years, these calves grow into strong cows or oxen, which can easily free themselves from the strong ropes.

However, these animals still continue to believe that they cannot break free from the strong ropes. So, they continue to remain 'imprisoned' because they still believe that they don't have the strength to overpower the chains. In fact, these poor animals will not even try to leave their shed if it was on fire because they believe that they 'cannot' break free from the rope.

This state of mind exists for many of us. Old and irrelevant beliefs stop us from moving forward and achieving our best potential. Follow these steps and the script for self-hypnosis:

Sit or lie down comfortably. Make sure your hands and legs are totally free. Don't hold on to anything.

Also, don't cross your legs or hands. Let your hands lie on either side of your body if you are lying down, and on your lap, if you are sitting.

Now, close your eyes and focus on your breath. As you relax, say the following script to yourself. Therefore, it would be best if you can memorize it beforehand. Else, you can record the script in your own voice and play it as you sit for your self-hypnosis sessions. So, here's the script for you:

- I am getting into a state of relaxation. Slowly my whole body and mind are going to relaxation mode. I am getting deeper into a calm state as each and every cell and muscle is relaxing completely. Everything is quiet and peaceful.
- The muscles on my face and neck are relaxing, relaxing, relaxing.
- The muscles of my face are loosening up and relaxing slowly.
- My hands are totally free and are in a relaxed state.
- My chest and stomach are in a relaxed state.
- My hips are relaxing.
- My thighs, knees, and calf muscles are relaxing.
- My ankles and heels are slowly relaxing and settling down.
- My feet are relaxing.
- My entire body and mind are completely relaxed. I am feeling calm and reposed from head to toe. I am ready to connect with my subconscious mind.

Once you are completely relaxed and calm, you can repeat the following affirmation for self-improvement. Use self-hypnosis to become a better version of yourself, and slowly but surely achieve self-actualization.

In the hypnotic trance, you can make self-suggestions to improve your emotional quotient, self-awareness, self-confidence, and self-esteem. Famous achievers like Winston Churchill, Thomas Edison, Albert Einstein, etc. used hypnosis to achieve great levels in their respective domains. Even sportspeople like Tiger Woods use hypnosis to achieve peak performance.

Self-hypnosis can help you improve yourself in different ways including better handling of emotions, increased productivity, and more so that you can lead a healthier, happier life than before.

Chapter Five: Self-Hypnosis Techniques and Precautions to be taken

This chapter is dedicated to giving you various techniques that help you get into a self-hypnosis mode. It also gives you some precautions you must take to prevent injury during your self-hypnosis session.

Before you start any session, remember to first focus on your breath to calm yourself down. Use short breaths for inhalation and let your exhalations be long and deep. Focusing on your breath is one of the most effective ways of priming your body and mind to relax completely and get into a trance-like calm state.

Self-Hypnosis Audio

You can choose from among the numerous self-hypnosis audio that is abundantly available in the market. Some are even available for free on the Internet. Find a couple of your favorites and use them to get into the self-hypnosis mode. Primarily, these audio files are recorded voices of professional hypnotherapist that facilitate the process of getting into the relaxed, hypnotic state.

Create Your Own Audio

If you cannot find audio of your choice or prefer to listen to the sound of your own voice, then you can create your own audio file, which you can play for your self-hypnosis session. Alternately, if you like the sound of your friend's voice, you can use his or her voice to record the self-hypnosis audio.

Write Down and Memorize Your Hypnotic Suggestions

As you already know, self-hypnosis works excellently for different needs and requirements. For every requirement, you need to have powerful hypnotic suggestions ready so that you can feed your subconscious mind appropriately. Therefore, you must create powerful, positive suggestions and write them down so that you don't forget them. Also, memorize them to ensure a seamless self-hypnotic session instead of having to take a peek at them while in your session.

Research the Internet for Hypnotic Gurus

Sometimes, when the conventional methods don't seem to work for you, it might make sense to research on the Internet for hypnotic gurus who employ traditional but powerful methods to facilitate hypnosis for their clients. Not only will you learn about new techniques but you will also be able to see how things work. You could see what mistakes you are making in your self-hypnosis session and make improvements.

Learn and Master Slow Yoga

The original form of yoga is primarily focused on bringing the body and mind in sync with one another so that your entire being is connected as a single entity. This state is also an excellent starting point for self-hypnosis. So, you can learn and master slow yoga and indulge in it regularly. You can have your self-hypnosis session immediately following the yoga session. Remember we are talking about the original yoga with Indian roots and not the hyped-up weight-loss-based westernized version.

Take Meditation Classes

Meditation is a great form of self-hypnosis, or rather, it is the first step towards becoming an effective self-hypnotizer. Therefore, it might make sense to spend some time and energy to take meditation classes from a qualified and reputed school or teacher. When you learn to meditate effectively, you are essentially making it easier for yourself to get into a hypnotic trance. Also, you can add positive self-suggestions during your meditation sessions.

Use Binaural Beats

Binaural beats help to change your brain waves into a different state that facilitates achieving a hypnotic state. Binaural beats are great for meditation and trance. It is best to use binaural beats that take your brain waves into the theta wavelength. At this stage, the brain is in its most receptive form, and self-suggestion can be easily and effectively made.

Use Sounds of Nature

Other sounds that help you get into a hypnotic state include sounds of nature like flowing water, rustling leaves, the sound of the ocean or sea waves, gentle rain, etc. You can use these kinds of sounds too for your hypnotic session. Let it play in the background as you self-hypnotize.

Use Your Favorite Soothing Instrumental Music

Piano, flute, or other kinds of soothing instrumental music playing in the background can also help you achieve a hypnotic state. Here are some lesser known instruments that have the power to create a calming, soothing environment:

Hammered dulcimer – It is a folk instrument steeped in the history of the Middle Ages.

Gong – When played skillfully, the gong is one of the most soothing musical instruments. It is commonly used during yoga sessions and even in Buddhist temples.

Wind Chimes – Spanning back to the ancient cultures, wind chimes are used in Feng Shui to maximize the flow of energy or chi. They are able to transmit beautiful melodies and sounds that aid in relaxation.

Other instruments suitable for meditation and self-hypnosis sessions include didgeridoo, tuning fork, etc. Use what you like best and help your body and mind relax totally and completely.

And finally, a word of caution. It is imperative that you don't try to do self-hypnosis when you are handling heavy machinery or driving or doing an activity that could lead to injury if you lose focus from the task. Always use self-hypnosis in a safe environment.

Conclusion

Self-hypnosis has the power to change your life for the better, helping you keep better control over your emotions and improving self-awareness. It would be wise to say that self-hypnosis might not be the ultimate solution for everyone's problems.

However, it can definitely be part of a solution for most life problems ranging from anxiety and depression to overcoming sleep and over-eating issues in your life.

The best thing about self-hypnosis is that you control and take charge of your life as per your needs and desires. However, while understanding the concept of self-hypnosis is easy, practicing and mastering it takes time, effort, and a lot of patient perseverance.

Use one of the many techniques mentioned in this book and ensure you practice every day. Perfection comes with repeated practice, and you will see that hypnotizing yourself to make positive changes in your life becomes a great habit that is deeply embedded in your psyche.

So, go ahead, use the techniques given in this book, and leverage the multiple benefits of self-hypnosis.

Resources

https://www.drmiller.com/learning-center/selfhypnosis/

https://www.skillsyouneed.com/ps/self-hypnosis.html

https://gshypnosis.com/hack-your-mind-with-hypnosis-to-motivate-and-increase-ambition/

https://anaheimlighthouse.com/blog/does-hypnosis-work-for-drug-addiction/

https://www.self-help-and-self-development.com/self-hypnosis-script.html

https://bebrainfit.com/self-hypnosis/

https://lonerwolf.com/sound-healing-therapy/